Poetry

Songs I Sing to Myself

By

Omer Toledano

~

Dedicated to the One I Love

~

The Pure Infant

by

Omer Toledano

It has become contaminated

Trying to push back the dirt

I cleanse myself

Almost like an infant

On the day of its birth

Not a spec of dust

Or pollution

Clean

Pure

No past

Just dirt awaiting to latch on

I re-awaken

Only to find pollution

And I weep silently

Like a baby

I long to find my way again

To be in the place

To be pure

To be timeless

Without a spec of dust

Without the dirt

Thrust upon me by time

There I remain

For you

To come back

~

The Void

by

Omer Toledano

In the void between sound

Two worlds collided

They danced and they swirled

Together abided

Primordial rhythm

Was the path unto them

And within it the rock

Which was to be their gem

In what seemed like a year

Will last for a lifetime

Throughout eons will echo

As we hear the night chime

It will arise and subside

As this wave always has

And continue this play

This sonic of jazz

In the void between worlds

There is nothing to see

There is nothing to hear

There is nowhere to be

You know it is there

And you know it is not

It is just in between

Where you seem to be caught

It will come it will go

And what you need to know

You will find out through time

And in time it will show

What needs to be shown

And to you will appear

Could be space

Could be time

Or the one you hold dear

In the void is where you
Feel most comfortable being
Where you talk with yourself
Where you're actually seeing
Out there is just show
They are not in the know
Of the things that are real
And which help you to grow

I am that I am
I am bliss overjoyed
I am truth I am found
In this infinite void

~

Expectation

by

Omer Toledano

It's my past which has shown me

What to expect

In this way which I live

I must pass

And reject

In this way which they live

They come to expect

What should be

Must be done

And how one must act

In this way how they judge

And draw their conclusion

Based on lies

Not the truth

Just their simple delusion

It's how they are built

It's how they are wired

So you know if you're in

So you know if you're hired

And this is the essence

Of this grand design

Are you with him?

Or are you still mine?

Either way it won't matter

The answer you know

As for I with the truth

Of you I let go

And continue to do so

Time after time

And write poems about it

Rhyme after rhyme

~

The Voices

by

Omer Toledano

The voices keep telling me

That I know nothing of love

It tells me to stay away

That I do not belong in this realm

Every fiber in my being says "Don't do this!"

"Go home! Relieve yourself."

The voice tells me that it is true

It is not for me

It is a mess

Even the strongest like yourself

Fail to keep balance

One big delusion created

To maintain momentum

Perpetuation

To keep the wheel in motion

It is not for you

Sit in the back seat

And enjoy the scenery

~

The Formless Rabbit

by

Omer Toledano

Once there was a formless rabbit

Who liked routine, order and habit

Every morning went on foot

And pulled a carrot from the root

And this went on for quite a while

This was just the rabbit's style

And so one day, the rabbit woke

And saw this thing was quite a joke

Pulling carrots from the ground

To and fro without a sound

And so the rabbit did agree

That eating carrots should be free

No more effort to this deed

Just the planting of a seed

And so the rabbit thought and thought
Of everything that he'd been taught
And then it came in quite a flash
The rabbit knew what he must do
To whip another by the lash
And so the rabbit brought his friend
To pick his carrots till the end
But now the rabbit reigned supreme
Alone atop this corrupt scheme
And this continued till the end
Our formless rabbit did not bend
Wanted just to move ahead
Blind to all as light of day
Pushing sideways on the way
And finally when he had topped
Breathed his last breath
And to death he dropped

But formless rabbit was not done

For now he was with nature one

And quicker than he knew what hit him

Faster than his lifeless rhythm

He looked around

Began to stare

Formless rabbit was now a bear

~

Miracle of the Tow Cable

by

Omer Toledano

In the darkness of night

A voice whispers

"I am here with you, always"

Remember the miracle of the tow cable

You entered the clearing in the forest

And when you needed it

It was there on the ground

With no earthly business being there

Put your faith in what your eyes see

I put it there for you

I pulled you out of where you were

And I shall do so many more times over

My hand guides your path

Trust the process

Remember the miracle of the tow cable

~

Queen of the Aztecs

by

Omer Toledano

I'm the autumn, you're the spring
I'm the rain, you're the blossom
I'm a bird in mid flight
You're the flower in my sight

Yours the people of the sun
Mine the people of the moon
Both the people of the light
Both illuminating noon

Darkness chaos with no end
Has no place in our domain
No fear, suffering or pain
Only love and joy will reign

Identify the falls we must

To hasten cure in both we trust

And do what is forever right

You illuminating day

And I illuminating night

Epitome of all desire

You're my ice

You're my fire

My wings with you shall never tire

With you, my love, a frequent flyer

And hosts of heaven and the earth

Will gaze upon as we give birth

To all that was and that will be

They'll give their blessing

You and Me

I will promise here on end
To cherish, keep you and defend
With music sounding when you wake
And whisper when a dream you make
My heart is here for you to take
Like the still waters on a lake

You're the mission in my eye
You're the pinnacle so high
You're the prize which I have won
Sun and Moon
Together One

~

The Dead Sea Hotel

by

Omer Toledano

One morning she asked
If I want to come with her
Just her and myself
And her son and her sister

Happily I inclined
And accepted the charge
Didn't flinch didn't waver
Was as they say, large

I booked me a room
At the Dead Sea Hotel
What transpired thereafter
Nobody could tell

I bathed and I soaked

Down in the spa

Got a healthy massage

From an elderly ma

We had dinner and fun

In the Bedouin tent

I had chicken skewers

And I was content

After filling our bellies

We went and retired

Night was falling

And we were all tired

And as we were sitting

Alone in the room

Her face suddenly dropped

And I sensed the gloom

She told me that she

No longer felt well

With us

Here

At the Dead Sea Hotel

And more things were said

And as I lay there in bed

I thought and I wondered

What went on in that head

The sun rose next morning

And the place was so calm

The mountains, the air

And the sand on my palm

If only I thought

She could be here

Right now

Instead of thinking the what

The when and the how

And again on the terrace

Looking out from above

She was absent from this

And from that and from love

It was there that I kissed her

Just our lips were aligned

Only looking at her

She was not of sound mind

On the drive back to home

Nothing could be done

The verdict already passed

And in there it was gone

With her beautiful eyes

I could already tell

She left me once more

At the Dead Sea Hotel

~

The Silent Ceremony

by

Omer Toledano

On the Greek island of Rhodes

I looked at the waves crashing down on a pebble beach

The city on my right

The sun and you on my left

The Turkish mountains on the horizon

I looked at the mildly turbulent sea

And then I looked into your eyes and saw

the storm within

I looked back at the waves

And back at you

Your hair fluttering in the cool evening breeze

Your eyes piercing into my soul

The love of my life

Then back at the waves

Then back at you

Not a word was said

A silent ceremony

And that was the beginning of summer

~

His Heart Beats Only for You

by

Omer Toledano

Nothing can be done about it

The more he thought about it

The more he tried in vain to change the tune

To change the rhythm

On His schedule there is no other

Violins playing a familiar song

Of a man who once was and is no more

Whose heart beats only for you

It's all that is left of this poor soul

Just a heart and it beats only for you

It is all crystal clear

How a month passes, then a year

How he once whispered in your ear

All the things that you wanted to hear

Promises left with a tear

To flow on his cheek as the violins played

He is hurt, he is wounded

Like an animal left to gasp his last breath

To welcome death

To come and take him for he cannot go on living

For he knows that once there were two

And his heart beats only for you

~

Where Does the Wikipedian Fall?

by

Omer Toledano

The sky up above

The Earth down below

The valley runs deep

The river does flow

The flower in bloom

And this tree grows so tall

As he gazed out at them

He kept asking himself

Where does the Wikipedian fall?

And to every astronomer

And author a name

And to every king in existence

Whom the throne did he claim

To every painting and artist

With a place down the hall

He asked with a sigh

Where does the Wikipedian fall?

To every event that was dreary

And physical theory

Every book that was sold

And places so eery

Every music and lyric

Known to man's ears

Birds of the heavens

And bison and deers

And historical facts

And post-war pacts

And fictional figures

And theatrical acts

From the Hollywood sign

To China's Great Wall

He asked once again

Where does the Wikipedian fall?

And despite all he's done

He really did love it

Like the Gurus he followed

He was from the world

But not of it

He knew for a fact

That his knowledge was small

As that old man once said

We can't harness it all

He bears silent witness

As he answers the call

And continues to ask to this day

Where does the Wikipedian fall?

~

The Rosetta Stone

by

Omer Toledano

I am the one
Who holds it together
I am the master
In charge of the tether

I am the one
Entrusted with power
I am the one
Who holds up the tower

If it wasn't for I
It would all fall apart
If it wasn't for I
With the purple heart

Where they die all of them
The shy and the weak
Is where I come in
To combat the bleak
It takes courage to talk
It takes courage to walk
It takes courage to fight
And to hunt like a hawk

If I fall
They fall with me
And that cannot be
With their light and their goodness
They encircle me
So that one day I'd rise
And shield them from harm
But till then I bestow
Upon them my charm

I am the one
Who need not atone
I am the one
Who sets the tone
I am the one
I'm flesh and I'm bone
I am the only
Rosetta Stone

~

Collective Orgasm

by

Omer Toledano

Does the amoeba feel pleasure

When it multiplies

Does the tiny fungus gasp

When it releases its tiny spores

Does the flower get aroused

When the bee suckles the nectar while touching its
anthers

Does the tree sway in ecstasy

Before bearing fruit

In the words of the song

How does the spring know its time?

Does the mountain lion question anything

Before it mounts

Give and take

Take and give

Releasing excess

Recyclers of the universe we are

Taking in and spewing out

Magnificent creation

A brief enjoyable moment

A collective orgasm

In eternity

~

Made in the USA
Coppell, TX
13 January 2024

27569196R00023